How the Vote Was Won

How the Vote Was Won

A Play in One Act

Cicely Hamilton and
Christopher St. John

MINT EDITIONS

How the Vote Was Won: A Play in One Act was first published in 1913.

This edition published by Mint Editions 2021.

ISBN 9781513279961 | E-ISBN 9781513284989

Published by Mint Editions®

**MINT
EDITIONS**

minteditionbooks.com

Publishing Director: Jennifer Newens
Design & Production: Rachel Lopez Metzger
Project Manager: Micaela Clark
Typesetting: Westchester Publishing Services

On to her husband's coat. She is a pretty, fluffy little woman who could never be bad-tempered, but might be fretful. At this minute she is smiling indulgently, and rather irritatingly, at her sister WINIFRED, *who is sitting by the fire* (L.) *when the curtain rises, but gets up almost immediately to leave.* WINIFRED *is a tall and distinguished looking young woman with a cheerful, capable manner and an emphatic diction which betrays the public speaker. She wears the colours of the National Woman's Social and Political Union.*

WINIFRED: Well, goodbye, Ethel. It's a pity you won't believe me. I wanted to let you and Horace down gently, or I shouldn't be here.

ETHEL: But you're always prophesying these dreadful things, Winnie, and nothing ever happens. Do you remember the day when you tried to invade the House of Commons from submarine boats? Oh, Horace, did laugh when he saw in the papers that you had all been landed on the Hovis wharf by mistake! "By accident, on purpose!" Horace said. He couldn't stop laughing all the evening. "What price your sister Winifred," he said, "She asked for a vote, and they gave her bread." He kept on—you can't think of how funny he was about it!

WINIFRED: Oh, but I can! I know my dear brother-in-law's sense of humour is his strong point. Well, we must hope it will bear the strain that is going to be put on it today. Of course, when his female relations invade his house—he may think it excruciatingly funny. One never knows.

ETHEL: Winnie, you're only teasing me. They would never do such a thing. They must know we have only one spare bedroom, and that's to be for a paying guest when we can afford to furnish it.

WINIFRED: The servants' bedroom will be empty. Don't forget that all the domestic servants have joined the League and are going to strike, too.

ETHEL: Not ours, Winnie. Martha is simply devoted to me, and poor little Lily *couldn't* leave. She had no home to go to. She would have to go to the workhouse.

WINIFRED: Exactly where she will go. All those women who have no male relatives, or are refused help by those they have, have instructions to go to the relieving officer. The number of female paupers who will pour through the workhouse gates tonight all over England will frighten the Guardians into blue fits.

ETHEL: Horace says you'll never *frighten* the Government into giving you the vote.

WINIFRED: It's your husband, your dear Horace, and a million other dear Horaces who are going to do the frightening this time. By tomorrow, perhaps, before, Horace will be marching to Westminister shouting out "Votes for Women!"

ETHEL: Winnie, how absurd you are! You know how often you've tried to covert Horace and failed. It is like that he will become a Suffragette just because—

WINIFRED: Just because—? Go on, Ethel

ETHEL: Well, you know—all this you've been telling me about his relations coming here and asking him to support them. Of course I don't believe it. Agatha, for instance, would never dream of giving up her situation. But if they did come Horace would just tell them he *couldn't* keep them. How could he on £4 a week?

WINIFRED: How could he! That's the point! He couldn't of course. That's why he'll want to get rid of them at any cost—even the cost of letting women have the Vote. That's why he and the majority of men in this country shouldn't for years have kept alive the foolish superstition that all women are support by men. For years we have told them it was a delusion, but they could not take our arguments seriously. Their method of answering us was exactly that of the little boy in the street who cries "Yah—Suffragette!" when he sees my ribbon.

ETHEL: I always wish you wouldn't wear it when you come here. . . Heroace does so dislike it. He thinks it unwomanly.

WINIFRED: Oh! Does he? Tomorrow he may want to borrow it—when he and the others have had their object lesson. They wouldn't listen to argument. . . so we had to expose their pious fraud about woman's place in the world in a very practical and sensible way. At this very minute working women of every grade in every part of England are ceasing work, and going to demand support and the necessities of life from their nearest male relatives, however distant the nearest relative may be. I hope, for your sake, Ethel, that Horace's relatives aren't an exacting lot!

ETHEL: There wasn't a word about it in the *Daily Mail* this morning.

WINIFRED: Never mind. The evening papers will make up for it.

ETHEL: What male relative are you going to, Winnie? Uncle Joseph?

CICELY HAMILTON AND CHRISTOPHER ST. JOHN

WINIFRED: Oh, I'm in the fighting line, as usual, so our dear uncle will be spared. My work is with the great army of women who have no male belongings of any kind! I shall be busy till midnight marshalling them to the workhouse. . . This is perhaps the most important part of the strike. By this we shall hit men as ratepayers even when they have escaped us as relatives! Every man, either in a public capacity or a private one, will find himself face to face with the appalling problem of maintaining millions of women in idleness. Will the men take up the burden, d'ye think? Not they! (*Looks at her watch*) Good heavens! The strike began ages ago. I must be off. I've wasted too much time here already.

ETHEL (*Looking at the clock*): I had no idea it was so late. I must see about Horace's tea. He may be home any minute. (*Rings the bell* L.)

WINIFRED: Poor Horace!

ETHEL (*Annoyed*): Why "poor Horace?" I don't think he has anything to complain of. (*Rings again*)

WINIFRED: I feel some pity at this minute for all men.

ETHEL: What can have happened to Martha?

WINIFRED: She's gone, my dear, that's all.

ETHEL: Nonsense. She's been with me ever since I was married, and I pay her very good wages.

(*Enter* LILY, *a shabby little maid-of-all-work, dressed for walking, the chief effect of the toilette being a very cheap and very smart hat*)

ETHEL: Where's Martha, Lily?

LILY: She's left, m'm.

ETHEL: Left! She never gave me notice.

LILY: No, m'm, we wasn't to give no notice, but at three o' clock we was to quit.

ETHEL: But why? Don't be a silly little girl. And you musn't come in here with your hat.

LILY: I was just goin' when you rang. That's what I've got me 'at for.

ETHEL: Going! Where? It's not your afternoon out.

LILY: I'm goin' back to the Union. There's dozens of others goin' with me.

ETHEL: But why—

LILY: Miss Christabel—she told us. She says to us:

"Now look 'ere, all of yer—you who've got no men to go to on Thursday—yer've got to go to the Union," she says; "and the one who 'angs back"—and she looked at me, she did—"may be the person 'oo the 'ole strain of the movement is restin' on, the traitor 'oo's sailin' under the 'ostile flag," she says; and I says, "That won't be me—not much!"

(*During this speech* WINIFRED *puts on a sandwich board which bears the inscription: "This way to the Workhouse"*)

WINIFRED: Well, Ethel, are you beginning to believe?

ETHEL: Oh, I think it's very unkind—very wicked. How am I to get Horace anything to eat with no servants?

WINIFRED: Cheer up, my dear. Horace and the others can end the strike when they choose. But they're going to have a jolly bad time first. Goodbye.

(*Exit* WINNIE, *singing the "Marseillaise"*)

LILY: Wait a bit, Miss. I'm comin' with yer (*Sings the "Marseillaise" too*)

ETHEL: No, no. Oh, Lily, please don't go, or at any rate bring up the kettle first, and the chops, and the frying pan. Please! Then I think I can manage.

LILY (*Coming back into the room and speaking impressively*): There's no ill feeling. It's objick lesson—that's all.

(*Exit* LILY. ETHEL *begins to cry weakly; then lays the table; gets bread, cruet, tea, cups, etc., from the cupboard* [R.]. LILY *re-enters with a frying pan, a kettle, and two raw chops*)

LILY: 'Ere you are—it's the best I can do. You see, mum, I've got to be recognised by the State. I don't think I'm a criminal nor a lunatic, and I oughtn't to be treated as sich.

ETHEL: You poor little simpleton. Do you suppose that, even if this absurd plan succeeds, *you* will get a vote?

LILY: I may—you never know your luck; but that's not why I'm giving up work. It's so as I shan't stop them as ought to 'ave it. The 'ole strain's on me, and I'm going' to the Union—so goodbye mum.

(*Exit* LILY)

ETHEL: And I've always been so kind to you! Oh, you little brute! What *will* Horace say? (*Looking out of the window*) It can't be true. Everything outside looks the same as usual. (HORACE's *voice outside*): We must have at least sixteen Dreadnoughts this year. (WILLIAMS' *voice*): You can't get 'em, old chap, unless you expect the blooming colonies to pay for 'em.) Ah, here is Horace, and Gerald Williams with him. Oh, I hope Horace hasn't asked him to tea! (*She powders her nose at the glass, then pretends to be busy with the kettle*)

(*Enter* HORACE COLE—*an English master in his own house—and* GERALD WILLIAMS, *a smug young man stiff with self consciousness*)

ETHEL: You're back early, aren't you, Horry? How do you do, Mr. Williams?

GERALD WILLIAMS: How do you do, Mrs. Cole? I just dropped in to fetch a book husband's promised to lend me.

(HORACE *rummages in bookshelves*)

ETHEL: Had a good day, Horry?

HORACE: Oh, must as usual. Ah, here it is (*Reading out the title*)—"Where's the Wash-tub now?" with a preface by Lord Curzon of Kedleston, published by the Men's League for Opposing Women's Suffrage. If that doesn't settle your missus, nothing will.

ETHEL: Is Mrs. Williams a Suffragette?

GERALD: Rather; and whenever I say anything, all she can answer is, "You know nothing about it." Thank you, old man. I'll read it to her after tea. So long. Goodbye, Mrs. Cole.

ETHEL: Did Mrs. Williams tell you anything this morning. . . before you went to the City? . . .

GERALD: About Votes for Women, do you mean? Oh, no. Not allowed at breakfast. In fact, not allowed at all. I tried to stop her going to these meetings where they fill the women's heads with all sorts of rubbish, and she said she'd give 'em up if I'd give up my footer matches; so we agreed to disagree. See you tomorrow, old chap. Goodbye, Mrs. Cole.

(*Exit* GERALD WILLIAMS)

HORACE: You might have asked him to stop to tea. You made him very welcome—I don't think.

ETHEL: I'm sorry; but I don't think he'd have stayed if I *had* asked him.

HORACE: Very likely not, but one should always be hospitable. Tea ready?

ETHEL: Not quite, dear. It will be in a minute.

HORACE: What on earth is all this!

ETHEL: Oh, nothing. I only thought I would cook your chop for you up here today—just for fun.

HORACE: I really think, Ethel, that so long as we can afford a servant, it's rather unnecessary.

ETHEL: You know you're always complaining of Martha's cooking. I thought you would like me to try.

HORACE: My dear child! It's very nice of you. But why not cook in the kitchen? Raw meat in the sitting room!

ETHEL: Oh, Horry, don't!

(*She puts her arms round his neck and sobs. The chop at the end of the toasting fork in her hand dangles in his face*)

HORACE: What on earth's the matter? Ethel, dear, don't be hysterical. If you knew what it was to come home fagged to death and be worried like this. . . I'll ring for Martha and tell her to take away these beastly chops. They're getting on my nerves.

ETHEL: Martha's gone.

HORACE: When? Why? I'd you have a row. I suppose you had to give her a month's wages. I can't afford that sort of thing, you know.

ETHEL (*Sobbing*): It's not you who afford it, anyhow. Don't I pay Martha out of my own money?

HORACE: Do you call it ladylike to throw that in my face. . .

ETHEL (*Incoherently*): I'm not throwing it in your face. . . but as it happens I didn't pay her anything. She went off without a word. . . and Lily's gone, too.

(*She puts her head down on the table and cries*)

HORRACEL: Well, that's a good riddance. I'm sick of her dirty face and slovenly ways. If she ever does clean my boots, she makes them look worse than when I took them off. We must try and get a charwoman.

ETHEL: We shan't be able to. Isn't it in the papers?

HORACE: What *are* you talking about?

ETHEL: Winifred said it would be in the evening papers.

HORACE: Winifred! She's been here, has she? That accounts for everything. How that woman comes to be your sister I can't imagine. Of course she's mixed up with this wildcat scheme.

ETHEL: Then you know it!

HORACE: Oh, I saw something about "Suffragettes on Strike" on the posters on my way home. Who cares if they do strike? They're no use to anyone. Look at Winifred. What does she ever do except go around making speeches, and kicking up a row outside the House of Commons until she forces the police to arrest her. Then she goes to prison and poses as a martyr. Martyr! We all know she could go home at once if she would promise the magistrate to behave herself. What they ought to do is try all these hysterical women in camera and sentence them to be ducked—privately. Then they'd soon give up advertising themselves.

ETHEL: Winnie has a splendid answer to that, but I forget what it is. Oh, Horry, was there anything on the posters about the nearest male relative?

HORACE: Ethel, my dear, you haven't gone dotty, have you? When you have quite done with my chair, I—(*He helps her out of the chair* C. *and sits down*) Thank you

ETHEL: Winnie said that not only are all the working women going to strike, but they are going to make their nearest male relatives support them.

HORACE: Rot!

ETHEL: I thought how dreadful it would be if Agatha came, or that cousin of yours on the stage whom you won't let me know, or your Aunt Lizzie! Martha and Lily have gone to *their* male relatives; at least, Lily's gone to the workhouse—it's all the same thing. Why should it be true? Oh, look, Horace, there's a cab—with luggage. Oh, what shall we do?

HORACE: Don't fuss! It's stopping next door, not here at all.

ETHEL: No, no; it's here. (*She rushes out*)

HORACE (*Calling after her*): Come back! You can't open the door yourself. It looks as if we didn't keep a servant.

(*Re-enter* ETHEL, *followed after a few seconds by* AGATHA. AGATHA *is a weary looking woman of about thirty-five. She wears the National Union colours, and is dowdily dress*)

ETHEL: It *is* Agatha—and such a big box. Where *can* we put it?

AGATHA (*Mildly*): How do you do, Horace. (*Kisses him*) Dear Ethel! (*Kisses her*) You're not looking so well as usual. Would you mind paying the cabman two shillings, Horace, and helping him with my box? It's rather heavy, but then it contains all my worldly belongings.

HORACE: Agatha—you haven't lost your situation! You haven't left the Lewises?

AGATHA: Yes, Horace; I left at three o'clock.

HORACE: My dear Agatha—I'm extremely sorry—but we can't put you up here.

AGATHA: Hadn't you better pay the cab? Two shillings so soon becomes two-and-six. (*Exit* HORACE) I am afraid my brother doesn't realize that I have some claim on him.

ETHEL: We thought you were so happy with the Lewises.

AGATHA: So were the slaves in America when they had kind masters. They didn't want to be free.

ETHEL: Horace said you always had late dinner with them when they had no company.

AGATHA: Oh, I have no complaint against my late employers. In fact, I was sorry to inconvenience them by leaving so suddenly. But I had a higher duty to perform than my duty to them.

ETHEL: I don't know what to do. It will worry Horace dreadfully.

(*Re-enter* HORACE)

HORACE: The cab *was* two-and-six, and I had to give a man twopence to help me in with that Noah's ark. Now, Agatha, what does this mean? Surely in your position it was very unwise to leave the Lewises. You can't stay here. We must make some arrangement.

AGATHA: Any arrangement you like, dear, provided you support me.

HORACE: I support you!

AGATHA: As my nearest male relative, I think you are obliged to do so. If you refuse, I must go to the workhouse.

HORACE: But why can't you support yourself? You've done it for years.

AGATHA: Yes—ever since I was eighteen. Now I am going to give up work, until my work is recognised. Either my proper place is the home—the home provided for me by some father, brother, husband, cousin or uncle—or I am a self-supporting member of the State who ought not to be shut out from the rights of citizenship.

HORACE: All this sounds as if you had become a Suffragette! Oh, Agatha, I always thought you were a lady.

AGATHA: Yes, I *was* a lady—such a lady that at eighteen I was thrown upon the world, penniless, with no training whatever which fitted me to earn my own living. When women become citizens I believe that daughters will be given the same chances as sons, and such a life as mine will be impossible.

HORACE: Women are so illogical. What on earth has all this to do with your planting yourself on me in this inconsiderate way? You put me in a most unpleasant position. You must see, Agatha, that I haven't the means to support a sister as well as a wife. Couldn't you go to some friends until you find another situation?

AGATHA: No, Horace. I'm going to stay with you.

HORACE (*Changing his tone and turning nasty*): Oh, indeed! And for how long—if I may ask?

AGATHA: Until the Bill for the removal of the sex disability is passed.

HORACE (*Impotently angry*): Nonsense. I can't keep you, and I won't. I have always tried to do my duty by you. I think hardly a week passes that I don't write to you. But now that you have deliberately thrown up an excellent situation as a governess and come here and threatened me—yes, threatened me—I think it's time to say that, sister or no sister, I will be master in my own house!

(*Enter* MOLLY, *a good looking young girl of about twenty. She is dressed in well-cut, tailor-made clothes, wears a neat little hat, and carries some golf clubs and a few books*)

MOLLY: How are you, Uncle Horace? Is that Aunt Aggie? How d'ye do? I haven't seen you since I was a kid.

HORACE: Well, what have you come for?

MOLLY: There's a charming welcome to give your only niece!

HORACE: You know perfectly well, Molly, that I disapprove of you in every way. I hear—I have never read it, of course—but I hear that you have written a most scandalous book. You live in lodgings by yourself, when if you chose you could afford some really nice and refined boarding house. You have most undesirable acquaintances, and altogether—

MOLLY: Cheer up, Uncle. Now's your chance of reforming me. I've come to live with you. You can support me and improve me at the same time.

HORACE: I never heard such impertinence! I have always understood from you that you earn more than I do.

MOLLY: Ah, yes; but you never *liked* my writing for money, did you? You called me "sexless" once because I said that as long as I could support myself I didn't feel an irresistible temptation to marry that awful little bounder Weekes.

ETHEL: Reginald Weekes! How can you call him a bounder! He was at Oxford.

MOLLY: Hullo, Auntie Ethel! I didn't notice you. You'll be glad to hear I haven't brought much luggage—only a night gown and some golf clubs.

HORACE: I suppose this a joke!

MOLLY: Well, of curse that's one way of looking at it. I' not going to support myself any longer. I'm going to be a perfect lady and depend on my Uncle Horace—my nearest male relative—for the necessities of life. (*A motor horn is heard outside*) Aren't you glad that I am not going to write another scandalous book, or live in lodgings by myself!

ETHEL (*At the window*): Horace! Horace! There's someone getting out of a motor—a grand motor. Who can it be? And there's no one to answer the door.

MOLLY: That doesn't matter. I found it open, and left it open to save trouble.

ETHEL: She's got luggage, too! The chauffeur's bringing in a dressing case.

HORACE: I'll turn her into the street—and the dressing case, too.

(*He goes fussily to the door and meets* MADAME CHRISTINE *on the threshold. The lady is dressed smartly and tastefully. Age about forty, manners elegant, smile charming, speech resolute. She carries a jewel case, and consults a legal document during her first remarks*)

MADAME C.: You are Mr. Cole?

HORACE: No! Certainly not! (*Wavering*) At least, I was this morning, but—

MADAME C.: Horace Cole, son of john Hay Cole, formerly of Streatham, where he carried on the business of a—

(*A motor horn sounds outside*)

HORACE: I beg your pardon, but my late father's business has really nothing to do with this matter, and to a professional man it's rather trying to have these things raked up against him. Excuse me, but do you want your motor to go?

MADAME C.: It's not my motor any longer; and—yes, I do want it go, for I may be staying here some time. I think you had one sister Agatha, and one brother Samuel, now dead. Samuel was much older than you—

AGATHA: Why don't you answer, Horace? Yes, that's perfectly correct. I am Agatha.

MADAME C.: Oh, are you? How d'ye do?

MOLLY: And Samuel Cole was my father.

MADAME C.: I'm very glad to meet you. I didn't know I had such charming relations. Well, Mr. Cole, my father was John Hay Cole's first cousin; so you, I think, are my second cousin, and my nearest male relative.

HORAC (*Distractedly*): If anyone calls me that again I shall go mad.

MADAME C.: I am afraid you aren't quite pleased with the relationship!

HORACE: You must excuse me—but I don't consider a second cousin exactly a relation.

MADAME C.: Oh, it answers the purpose. I suddenly find myself destitute, and I want you to support me. I am sure you would not like a Cole to go to the workhouse.

HORACE: I don't care a damn where any of 'em go.

ETHEL (*Shocked*): Horry! How can you!

MADAME C.: That's frank, at any rate; but I am sure, Cousin Horace, that in spite of your manners, your heart's in the right place. You won't refuse me board and lodging, until Parliament makes it possible for me to resume my work?

HORACE: My dear madam, do you realize that my salary is £3 10s. a week—and that my house will hardly hold your luggage, much less you?

MADAME C.: Then you must agitate. Your female relatives have supported themselves up till now, and asked nothing from you. I myself, dear cousin, was, until this morning, running a profitable dressmaking business in Hanover Square. In my public capacity I am Madame Christine.

MOLLY: I know! I've never been able to afford you.

HORACE: And do you think, Madame Christine—

MADAME C.: Cousin Susan, please.

HORACEL: Do you think that you are justified in coming to a poor clerk and asking him to support you—you could probably turn over my yearly income in a single week! Didn't you come here in your own motor?

MADAME C.: At three o'clock that motor became the property of the Women's Social and Political Union. All the rest of my property and all available cash have been divided equally between the National Union and the Women's Freedom League. Money is the sinews of war, you know.

HORACE: Do you mean to tell me that you've given all your money to the Suffragettes! It's a pity you haven't a husband. He'd very soon stop your doing such foolish things.

MADAME C.: I had a husband once. He liked me to do foolish things—for instance, to support him. After all that unfortunate experience, Cousin Horace, you may imagine how glad I am to find a man who really is a man, and will support me instead. By the way, I should *so* like some tea. Is the kettle boiling?

ETHEL (*Feebly*): There aren't enough cups! Oh what *shall* I do?

HORACE: Never mind, Ethel; I shan't want any. I am going to dine in town and go to the theatre. I shall hope to find you all gone when I come back. If not, I shall send for the police.

(*Enter* MAUDIE SPARK, *a young woman with aggressively cheerful manner, a voice raucous from much bellowing of music-hall songs, a hat of huge size, and a heart of gold*)

MAUDIE: 'Ullo! 'ullo! who's talking about the police? Not my dear cousin Horry!

HORACE: How dare you come here?

MAUDIE: Necessity, old dear. If I had a livelier male relative, you may bet I'd have gone to him! But you, Horace, are the only first cousin of this poor orphan. What are you in such a hurry for?

HORACE: Let me pass! I'm going to the theatre.

MAUDIE: Silly jay! the theaters are all closed—and the halls too. The actresses have gone on strike—resting indefinitely. I've done my little bit towards that. They won't get anymore work out of Maudie Spark, Queen of Comediennes, until the women have got the vote. Ladies and fellow-relatives, you'll be pleased to hear the strike's going fine. The big drapers can't open tomorrow. One man can't fill the place of fifteen young ladies at once, you see. The duchesses are out in the streets begging people to come in and wash their kids. The City men are trying to get taxi-men to do their typewriting. Every man, like Horry here, has his house full of females. Most of 'em thought, like Horry, that they' go to the theatre to escape. But there's not a blessed theatre to go to! Oh, what a song it'll make. "A woman's place is the home—I don't think, I don't think, I don't think."

HORACE: Even if this is not a plot against me personally, even if there are other women in London at this minute disgracing their sex—

MAUDIE: Here, stop it—come off it! If it comes to that, what are *you* doing—threatening your womankind with the police and the workhouse.

HORACE: I was not addressing myself to you.

AGATHA: Why not, Horace? She's your cousin. She needs your protection just as much as we do.

HORACE: I regard that woman as the skeleton in the cupboard of a respectable family; but that's neither here nor there. I address myself to the more ladylike portion of this gathering, and I say that whatever is going on, the men will know what to do, and will do it with dignity and firmness. (*The impressiveness of this statement is marred by the fact that* HORACE'S *hand, emphasising it, comes down heavily on the loaf of bread on the table*) A few exhibitions of this kind won't frighten them.

MAUDIE: Oh, won't it! I like that! They're being so firm and so dignified that they're running down to the House of Commons like lunatics, and black guarding the Government for not having given us the vote before! (*Shouts of outside newsboys in the distance*)

MOLLY: Splendid! Have they begun already?

MADAME C.: Get a paper, Cousin Horace. I know some men never believe anything till they see it in the paper.

ETHEL: They boys are shouting out something now. Listen.

(*Shouts outside. "Extry special. Great strike of women. Women's strike. Theatres closed. Extry special edition. Star! News! 6:30 edition!"*)

MOLLY: You see. Since this morning Suffragettes have become women!

ETHEL (*At window*): Here, boy, paper!

(*Cries go on. "Extra special Star. Men petition the Government. Votes for Women. Extry special"*)

Oh, heavens, here's Aunt Lizzie!

(*As* ETHEL *pronounces the name* HORACE *dives under the table. Enter* AUNT LIZZIE *leading a fat spaniel and carrying a bird cage with a parrot in it.* MISS ELIZABETH WILKINS *is a comfortable, middle-aged body of a type well known to those who live in the less fashionable quarter of Bloomsbury. She looks as if she kept lodgers, and her looks do not belie her. She is not very well educated, but has a good deal of native intelligence. Her features are homely and her clothes about thirty years behind the times*)

AUNT L.: Well, dears, all here? That's right. Where's Horace? Out? Just as well; we can talk more freely. I'm sorry I'm late but animals do so hate a move. It took a long time to make them understand the strike. But I think they will be very comfortable here. You love dogs, don't you Ethel?

ETHEL: Not Ponto. He always growls at me.

AUNT L.: Clever dog! he knows you don't sympathise with the cause.

ETHEL: But I do, Aunt; only I have always said that as I was happily married I thought it had very little to do with me.

AUNT L.: You've changed your mind about today, I should think! What a day it's been! We never expected everything would go so smoothly. They say the Bill's to be rushed through at once. No more broken promises, no more talking out; deeds, not words, at last! Seen the papers? The press are not boycotting us today, my dears (MADAME C., *and* MAUDIE *each take a paper*) The boy who sold them to me put the money back into Ponto's collecting box. That dog must have made five pounds for the cause since this morning.

(HORACE *puts his head out and says* "Liar!")

MOLLY: Oh, do listen to this. It's too splendid! (*Reading from the paper*) "Women's Strike—Latest: Messrs. Lyons and Co. announce that by special arrangement with the War Office the places of their defaulting waitresses will be filled by the non-commissioned officers and men of the 2nd Battalion Coldstream Guard. Business will therefore be carried on as usual."

MADAME C.: What do you think of this? (*Reading*) "Latest Intelligence.—It is understood that the Naval Volunteers have been approached by the authorities with the object of inducing them to the act of charwomen of the House of Commons."

AUNT L. (*To* ETHEL): Well, my dear! Read, then, what the *Star* says.

ETHEL (*Tremulously reading*): "The queue of women waiting for admission to the Westminster workhouse is already a mile and a half in length. As the entire police force are occupied in dealing with the men's processions, Lord Escher has been approached with a view to ascertaining if the Territorials can be sworn in as special constables."

MAUDIE (*Laughing*): This is a little bit of all right. (*Reading*) "Our special representative, on calling upon the Prime Minister with the object of ascertaining his views on the situation, was informed that the Right Honourable gentleman was unable to receive him, as he was actively engaged in making his bed with the assistance of the boot-boy and a Foreign Office messenger."

AUNT L.: Always unwilling to receive people, you see! Well, he must be feeling sorry now that he never received us. Everyone's putting the blame on to him. It's extraordinary how many men—and newspapers, too—have suddenly found out that they have always been in favour of woman's suffrage! That's the sensible attitude, of course. It would be humiliating for them to confess that it was not until we held a pistol to their heads that they changed their minds. Well, at this minute I would rather be the man who has been our

CICELY HAMILTON AND CHRISTOPHER ST. JOHN

ally all along than the one who has been our enemy. It's not the popular thing to be "anti" any more. Any man who tries to oppose us today is likely to be slung up to the nearest lamp post.

ETHEL (*Rushing wildly to the table*): Oh, Horry! my Horry! (HORACE *comes out from under the table*)

AUNT L.: Why, bless the boy, what are you doing there?

HORACE: Oh, nothing. I merely thought I might be less in the way here, that's all.

AUNT L.: You didn't hide when I came in by any chance!

HORACE: I hide from you! Aren't you always welcome in this house?

AUNT L.: Well, I haven't noticed it particularly; and I'm not calling today, you understand, I've come to stay (HORACE, *dashed and beaten, begins to walk up and down the room, and consults* ETHEL) Well, well! I won't deny it was a wrench to leave 118a, Upper Montagu Place, old and young, gents and ladies, for twenty-five years—and no complaints! A home from home, they call it. All my ladies had left before I started out, on the same business as all of us—but what those poor boys will do for their dinner tonight I don't know. They're a helpless lot! Well, it's all over; I've given up my boarding-house, and I depend on you, Horace, to keep me until I am admitted to citizenship. It may take a long time.

HORACE: It must *not* take a long time! I shan't allow it. It shall be done at once. Well, you needn't all look so surprised. I know I've been against it, but I didn't realize things. I thought only a few howling dervishes wanted the vote; but when I find that you— Aunt—Fancy a woman of your firmness of character, one who has always been so careful of her money, being declared incapable of voting! The thing is absurd.

MADUIE: Bravo! Our Horry's waking up.

HORACE (*Looking at her scornfully*): If there are a few women here and there who *are* incapable—I mention no names, mind—it doesn't affect the position. What's going to be done? Who's going to do it? If this rotten Government think we're going to maintain millions of women in idelness just because they don't like the idea of my Aunt Lizzie making a scratch on a bit of paper and shoving it into a ballot box once every five years, this Government have reckoned without men—(*General cheering*) I'll show em' what I've got a vote for! What do they expect? You can't all marry. There aren't enough men to go round, and if you're earning your own living and paying taxes you ought to have a say; it's only fair. (*General cheering and a specially emphatic "Hear, hear" from* MADAME CHRISTINE) The Government are narrow-minded idiots! (MADAME C.: Hear! hear!) They talk as if all the women ought to stay at home washing and ironing. Well, before a woman has a wash-tub, she must have a home to put them in, mustn't she? And who's going to give it to her? I'd like them to tell me that. Do they expect *me* to do it? (AGATHA: Yes, dear) I say if she can do it herself and keep herself, who are the Government? They're only representing me, and being paid thousands a year by *me* for carrying out *my* wishes. (MOLLY: Oh, er-what ho! HORACE *turns on her angrily*) I like a woman to be a woman—that's the way I was brought up; but if she insists on having a vote—and apparently she does (ALL: She does! she does!) I don't see why she shouldn't have it. Many a woman came in here at the last election and tried to wheedle me into voting for her particular candidate. If she has time to do that—and I never heard the member say then that she ought to be at home washing the baby—I don't see why she hasn't time to vote. It's never taken up much of *my* time, or interfered with *my* work. I've only voted once in my life—but that's neither here nor there. I know what the vote does for me. It gives me a status; that's what you women want—a status. (ALL: Yes, yes; a status) I might even call it a *locus standi*. If I go now and tell these rotten Cabinet Ministers what I think of them, it's my *locus standi*—(MAUDIE: That's a good word)—that will force them to listen to me. Oh, I know. And, by gum! I'll give them a bit of my mind. They shall hear a few home truths for once. "Gentlemen." I shall say-well, that won't be true of all of them to start with, but one must give 'em the benefit of the doubt—"gentlemen, the men of England are sick and tired of your policy. Who's driven the women of England into this? *You*—(*He turns round on* ETHEL, *who jumps violently*)—because you were too stupid to know that they meant business—because you couldn't read the writing on the all. (*Hear, hear*) It may be nothing to you, gentlemen, that every industry in this country is paralysed and every Englishman's home turned into a howling wilderness—(MOLLY: Draw it mild, Uncle) A howling wilderness, I repeat—by your refusal to see what's as plain as the nose on your face; but I would have you know, gentlemen, that it *is* something

CICELY HAMILTON AND CHRISTOPHER ST. JOHN

to us. We aren't slaves. We never will be slaves—(AGATHA: Never, never!)—and we insist on reform. Gentlemen, conditions have changed, and women have to work. Don't mean encourage them to work, *invite* them to work? (AGATHA: Make them work) And women are placed in the battle of life on the same terms as we are, short of one thing, the *locus standi* of a vote. (MAUDIE: Good old *locus standi*!) If you aren't going to give it them, gentlemen, and if they won't go back to their occupations without it, we ask you, how they're going to live? Who's going to support them? Perhaps you're thinking of giving them old age pensions and asking the country to pay the piper! The country will see you damned first, if, gentlemen, you'll pardon the expression. It's dawning upon us all that the women would never have taken such a step as this if they hadn't been the victims of gross injustice. (ALL: Never) Why shouldn't they have a voice in the laws which regulate the price of food and clothes? Don't they pay for their food and clothes? (MAUDIE: Paid for mine all my life) Why shouldn't they have a voice in the rate of wages and the hours of labour in certain industries? Aren't they working at those industries? Aren't they working at those industries? If you had a particle of common sense or decent feeling, gentlemen—"

(*Enter* GERALD WILLIAMS *like a souvenir of Mafeking night. He shouts incoherently and in a hoarse voice. He is utterly transformed from the meek, smug being of an hour before. He is wearing several ribbons and badges and carrying a banner bearing this inscription: "The men of Brixton demand votes for women this evening"*)

WILLIAMS: Cole! Cole! Come on! Come on! You'll be late. The procession's forming up at the town hall. There's no time to lose. What are you slacking for? Perhaps this isn't good enough for you. I've got twelve of them in my drawing room. We shall be late for the procession if we don't start at once. Hurry up! Come on! Votes for women! Where's your banner? Where's your badge? Down with the Government! Rule Britannia! Votes for Women! D'you want to support a dozen women for the rest of your life, or don't you? Every man in Brixton is going to Westminster. Borrow a ribbon and come along. Hurry up, now! Hooray! (*Rushes madly out crying "Votes for Women!" Rule Britannia; Women never, never shall be slaves! Votes for Women!*)

(*All the women who are wearing ribbons decorate* HORACE)

ETHEL: My hero! (*She throws her arms round him*)

HORACE: You may depend on me—all of you—to see justice done. When you want a thing done, get a man to do it! Votes for Women!)

(AGATHA *gives him a flag, which he waves triumphantly*)

(*Curtain tableteau*: HORACE *marching majestically out of the door, with the women cheering him enthusiastically*)

CURTAIN

Note About the Author

Cicely Hamilton (1872–1952) was born as Cicely Hammill in 1872 in Paddington, London. She was taken in by foster parents after her mother disappeared. After becoming an actress, Cicely changed her last name to Hamilton to protect her family's privacy. Not only was Hamilton an actress, she was also a writer, journalist and feminist who aided in the struggle for women's suffrage in the United Kingdom. She founded the Women Writers Suffrage League with Bessie Hatton in 1908, which hosted many other famous women of literature, all in effort of obtaining rights for women and making their plight known. Hamilton wrote the famous suffrage song *The March of the Women*. Hamilton also wrote for magazines and freelanced as a journalist, informing the public about birth control and other rights women deserved. During World War I, she aided as a nurse and then as a performer to keep up morale amongst troops. Cicely Hamilton died in 1952 as an accomplished writer, actress and prominent figure for women's rights.

Christopher St. John (1871–1960) was a British author, playwright, and activist. Born Christabel Gertrude Marshal, St. John changed her name after her conversion to Catholicism in 1912. While studying to become a dramatist, St. John moved in with her boss's daughter, Edith Craig, and the two quickly became an inseparable couple. Later, an artist named Clare Atwood also joined the relationship, which the three maintained for the entirety of their adult lives. Passionate about the women's suffrage, St. John worked with other prominent leaders, writing articles and creating feminist literature to raise awareness and morale for the movement.

A Note from the Publisher

Spanning many genres, from non-fiction essays to literature classics to children's books and lyric poetry, Mint Edition books showcase the master works of our time in a modern new package. The text is freshly typeset, is clean and easy to read, and features a new note about the author in each volume. Many books also include exclusive new introductory material. Every book boasts a striking new cover, which makes it as appropriate for collecting as it is for gift giving. Mint Edition books are only printed when a reader orders them, so natural resources are not wasted. We're proud that our books are never manufactured in excess and exist only in the exact quantity they need to be read and enjoyed.

bookfinity™

Discover more of your favorite classics with Bookfinity™.

- Track your reading with custom book lists.
- Get great book recommendations for your personalized Reader Type.
- Add reviews for your favorite books.
- AND MUCH MORE!

Visit **bookfinity.com** and take the fun Reader Type quiz to get started.

Enjoy our classic and modern companion pairings!

Classic & Modern